The United States Presidents

Dwight D. EISENHOWER

Tamara L. Britton

Big Buddy Books
An Imprint of Abdo Publishing
abdopublishing.com

abdopublishing.com

Published by Abdo Publishing, a division of ABDO, PO Box 398166, Minneapolis, Minnesota 55439.
Copyright © 2017 by Abdo Consulting Group, Inc. International copyrights reserved in all countries. No
part of this book may be reproduced in any form without written permission from the publisher. Big Buddy
Books™ is a trademark and logo of Abdo Publishing.

Printed in the United States of America, North Mankato, Minnesota
062016
092016

Design: Sarah DeYoung, Mighty Media, Inc.
Production: Mighty Media, Inc.
Editor: Paige Polinsky
Cover Photograph: Getty
Interior Photographs: AP Images (pp. 7, 9, 17, 27); Corbis (pp. 5, 7, 11, 13, 21, 25);
    Getty Images (pp. 6, 15, 19, 23, 29)

Cataloging-in-Publication Data

Names: Britton, Tamara L., author.
Title: Dwight D. Eisenhower / by Tamara L. Britton.
Description: Minneapolis, MN : Abdo Publishing, [2017] | Series: United States
    presidents | Includes bibliographical references and index.
Identifiers: LCCN 2015957282 | ISBN 9781680780918 (lib. bdg.) |
    ISBN 9781680775112 (ebook)
Subjects: LCSH: Eisenhower, Dwight D. (Dwight David), 1890-1969--Juvenile
    literature. | Presidents--United States--Biography--Juvenile literature. |
    United States--Politics and government--1953-1961--Juvenile literature.
Classification: DDC 973.921/092 [B]--dc23
LC record available at http://lccn.loc.gov/2015957282

Contents

Dwight D. Eisenhower

General Dwight D. Eisenhower was the thirty-fourth US president. He was also a successful military leader. Eisenhower was a commander during **World War II**. After the war, he became the chief of the US Army.

Eisenhower was elected president in 1952. He was the first **Republican** president in 20 years. American businesses did well under Eisenhower's leadership. Citizens liked him and the peaceful way he ran the country.

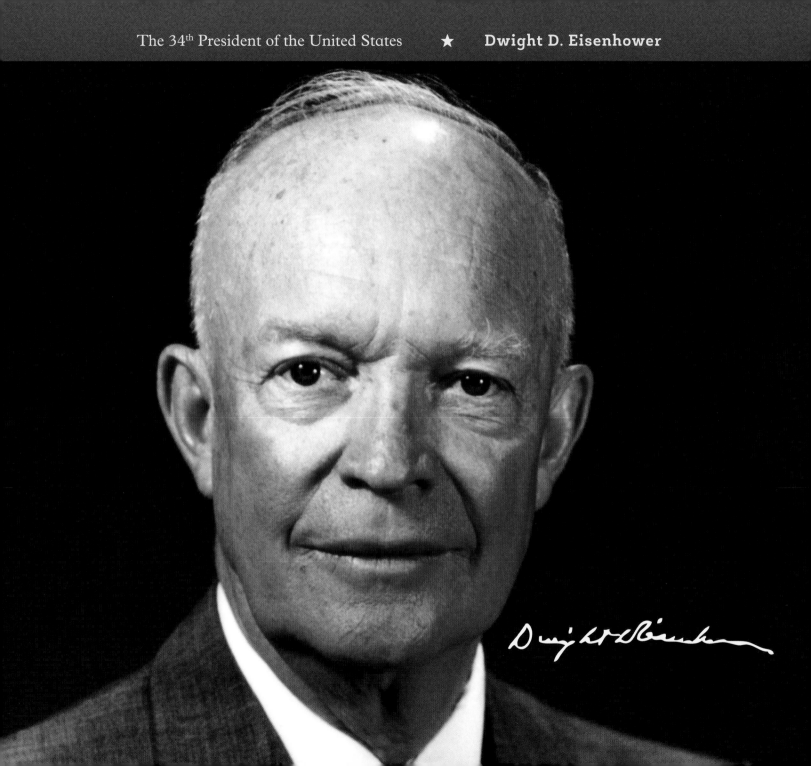

Timeline

1890
Dwight David Eisenhower was born on October 14 in Denison, Texas.

1945
Eisenhower was named chief of the US Army.

1942
Eisenhower was sent to London, England, to command US forces in Europe.

1952
On November 4, Eisenhower was elected the thirty-fourth president.

1957
Eisenhower signed the **Civil Rights** Act of 1957.

1956
Eisenhower was reelected US president.

1969
Dwight D. Eisenhower died on March 28.

7

Young Dwight

Dwight David Eisenhower was born on October 14, 1890, in Denison, Texas. His parents were David and Ida. When Dwight was two, his family moved to Kansas. Dwight was a good student. After finishing high school, he worked to support his family.

★ FAST FACTS ★

Born: October 14, 1890

Wife: Marie "Mamie" Doud (1896–1979)

Children: two

Political Party: Republican

Age at Inauguration: 62

Years Served: 1953–1961

Vice President: Richard Nixon

Died: March 28, 1969, age 78

Dwight (*far left*) with his family.
His five brothers were Arthur, Edgar,
Roy, Earl, and Milton.

Starting a Family

In 1911, Eisenhower entered the US Military **Academy** at West Point in New York. He often got into trouble there. Still, Eisenhower completed the program in 1915.

The US Army sent Eisenhower to San Antonio, Texas. There, he met Marie "Mamie" Doud. They married on July 1, 1916. That same day, Eisenhower was made first **lieutenant**.

In 1917, the Eisenhowers had a son. They named him Doud. Sadly, at three years old, Doud became ill and died.

After Doud's death, Eisenhower sent Mamie flowers each year on the child's birthday.

Military Man

Eisenhower became a captain in 1917. Throughout 1918, he trained soldiers in Gettysburg, Pennsylvania. For this work, Eisenhower was made a major in 1920.

In 1922, Eisenhower was stationed in the Philippines. Mamie stayed in the United States. That same year, she and Eisenhower welcomed another son, John.

Eisenhower worked under General Douglas MacArthur in the 1930s. But, Eisenhower wanted to command. His opportunity would soon arrive.

In the 1930s, Eisenhower (*right*) worked with General MacArthur in the Philippines.

World War II

In 1941, the United States entered **World War II**. Eisenhower soon became a general. In 1942, he traveled to London, England, to command US forces.

General Eisenhower led the successful attack on North Africa in July 1942. Army officials noticed Eisenhower's great leadership. So, in 1943, Eisenhower was named commander of the European **Allies**. He would lead Operation Overlord, an invasion of Western Europe.

Eisenhower helped his troops work together in North Africa. Their success made him a four-star general.

On June 6, 1944, Eisenhower's troops landed in Normandy, France. This first step in Operation Overlord is known as D-day. The operation was a great success.

On May 8, 1945, the Germans **surrendered**. The war ended several months later. The same year, Eisenhower became chief of the US Army.

In 1948, he left the army. Eisenhower became president of Columbia University in New York, New York. He also wrote a book about his time during the war.

★ DID YOU KNOW? ★

President Eisenhower was the first US president to govern all 50 states.

General Eisenhower directed his troops carefully before D-day. It only took them six days to secure the beach at Normandy.

A Strong Leader

In 1950, Eisenhower became commander of **NATO**. He was an able leader. So, Americans thought he would make a good president too.

On June 4, 1952, Eisenhower entered the presidential race. During this time, the United States was fighting the **Korean War**. Eisenhower promised to work for world peace.

Eisenhower was the **Republican** Party's choice. Senator Richard Nixon ran as his vice president. Eisenhower's main challenger was Adlai E. Stevenson.

While serving as commander of NATO, Eisenhower lived in Paris, France.

Peace Promise

On November 4, 1952, Eisenhower was elected the thirty-fourth president of the United States. He received nearly 34 million votes.

Eisenhower took office on January 20, 1953. Four weeks later, he went to Korea. On July 27, 1953, a peace agreement ended the **Korean War**. President Eisenhower had kept his promise.

★ DID YOU KNOW? ★

Eisenhower received more votes than any presidential candidate before him.

PRESIDENT EISENHOWER'S CABINET

First Term
January 20, 1953–January 20, 1957

- ★ **STATE:** John Foster Dulles
- ★ **TREASURY:** George M. Humphrey
- ★ **DEFENSE:** Charles E. Wilson
- ★ **ATTORNEY GENERAL:** Herbert Brownell Jr.
- ★ **INTERIOR:** Douglas McKay, Frederick A. Seaton (from June 8, 1956)
- ★ **AGRICULTURE:** Ezra Taft Benson
- ★ **COMMERCE:** Sinclair Weeks
- ★ **LABOR:** Martin P. Durkin, James P. Mitchell (from October 9, 1953)
- ★ **HEALTH, EDUCATION, AND WELFARE:** Oveta Culp Hobby (from April 11, 1953), Marion B. Folsom (from August 1, 1955)

Second Term
January 20, 1957–January 20, 1961

- ★ **STATE:** John Foster Dulles, Christian A. Herter (from April 22, 1959)
- ★ **TREASURY:** George M. Humphrey, Robert B. Anderson (from July 29, 1957)
- ★ **DEFENSE:** Charles E. Wilson, Neil H. McElroy (from October 9, 1957), Thomas S. Gates Jr. (from December 2, 1959)
- ★ **ATTORNEY GENERAL:** Herbert Brownell Jr., William P. Rogers (from January 27, 1958)
- ★ **INTERIOR:** Frederick A. Seaton
- ★ **AGRICULTURE:** Ezra Taft Benson
- ★ **COMMERCE:** Sinclair Weeks, Frederick H. Mueller (from August 10, 1959)
- ★ **LABOR:** James P. Mitchell
- ★ **HEALTH, EDUCATION, AND WELFARE:** Marion B. Folsom, Arthur S. Flemming (from August 1, 1958)

In the 1950s, a disease was harming millions of people. It was called **polio**. In 1955, a **cure** was found. Eisenhower and **Secretary of Health and Human Services** Oveta Hobby teamed up. They helped Americans receive the **remedy**.

Eisenhower also faced health problems of his own. In September 1955, he had a heart attack. It took him a few months to recover. By December, Eisenhower was well again. He was ready to run for reelection.

SUPREME COURT APPOINTMENTS

★ ★

Earl Warren: 1953

John Marshall Harlan: 1955

William J. Brennan Jr.: 1956

Charles Whittaker: 1957

Potter Stewart: 1958

Oveta Hobby
was the first
secretary of
health and
human services.

A Second Term

Eisenhower was reelected in 1956. At this time, many people worried about **Communism**. Eisenhower created a plan to aid nations that would fight its spread. Congress accepted the plan in 1957.

Meanwhile, African Americans were fighting for **civil rights.** At this time, children of different races were forced to attend separate schools. In 1954, the US government had decided to end this **segregation**. But many Southerners were unhappy with this decision.

When segregation ended at Central High School in Little Rock, Arkansas, Elizabeth Eckford was one of the school's first African-American students. She was mistreated by many of her white peers.

In Arkansas, nine African-American students joined Little Rock Central High School. White crowds tried to keep them out. Eisenhower sent soldiers to guard the new students. Later, Eisenhower signed the **Civil Rights** Act of 1957.

That same year, the Soviet Union sent the first **satellite** into space. In response, Eisenhower formed **NASA** in 1958. US pilots began flying over the Soviet Union. In 1960, the Soviets captured a US airplane. Eisenhower announced that the United States had been **spying** on the Soviet Union.

In 1959, Soviet leader Nikita Khrushchev (*left*) visited Eisenhower in the United States. After the US spying was discovered, Khrushchev refused to meet with Eisenhower again.

Home at Last

In 1951, a new law had been passed. It limited all presidents to two terms. Eisenhower was the first president required to follow this law. January 20, 1961, was his last day as president.

Eisenhower moved to his farm in Gettysburg, Pennsylvania. He raised animals, played golf, and spent time with family. On March 28, 1969, Dwight D. Eisenhower died. One of the last things he ever said was, "I've always loved my country."

Eisenhower was buried near his boyhood home in Abilene, Kansas.

Office of the President

Branches of Government

The US government has three branches. They are the executive, legislative, and judicial branches. Each branch has some power over the others. This is called a system of checks and balances.

★ Executive Branch

The executive branch enforces laws. It is made up of the president, the vice president, and the president's cabinet. The president represents the United States around the world. He or she also signs bills into law and leads the military.

★ Legislative Branch

The legislative branch makes laws, maintains the military, and regulates trade. It also has the power to declare war. This branch includes the Senate and the House of Representatives. Together, these two houses form Congress.

★ Judicial Branch

The judicial branch interprets laws. It is made up of district courts, courts of appeals, and the Supreme Court. District courts try cases. Sometimes people disagree with a trial's outcome. Then he or she may appeal. If a court of appeals supports the ruling, a person may appeal to the Supreme Court.

Qualifications for Office

To be president, a candidate must be at least 35 years old. The person must be a natural-born US citizen. He or she must also have lived in the United States for at least 14 years.

Electoral College

The US presidential election is an indirect election. Voters from each state choose electors. These electors represent their state in the Electoral College. Each elector has one electoral vote. Electors cast their vote for the candidate with the highest number of votes from people in their state. A candidate must receive the majority of Electoral College votes to win.

Term of Office

Each president may be elected to two four-year terms. The presidential election is held on the Tuesday after the first Monday in November. The president is sworn in on January 20 of the following year. At that time, he or she takes the oath of office.
It states:

> I do solemnly swear (or affirm) that I will faithfully execute the office of President of the United States, and will to the best of my ability, preserve, protect and defend the Constitution of the United States.

Line of Succession

The Presidential Succession Act of 1947 states who becomes president if the president cannot serve. The vice president is first in the line. Next are the Speaker of the House and the President Pro Tempore of the Senate. It may happen that none of these individuals is able to serve. Then the office falls to the president's cabinet members. They would take office in the order in which each department was created:

Secretary of State

Secretary of the Treasury

Secretary of Defense

Attorney General

Secretary of the Interior

Secretary of Agriculture

Secretary of Commerce

Secretary of Labor

Secretary of Health and Human Services

Secretary of Housing and Urban Development

Secretary of Transportation

Secretary of Energy

Secretary of Education

Secretary of Veterans Affairs

Secretary of Homeland Security

Benefits

★ While in office, the president receives a salary. It is $400,000 per year. He or she lives in the White House. The president also has 24-hour Secret Service protection.

★ The president may travel on a Boeing 747 jet. This special jet is called Air Force One. It can hold 70 passengers. It has kitchens, a dining room, sleeping areas, and more. Air Force One can fly halfway around the world before needing to refuel. It can even refuel in flight!

★ When the president travels by car, he or she uses Cadillac One. It is a Cadillac Deville that has been modified. The car has heavy armor and communications systems. The president may even take Cadillac One along when visiting other countries.

★ The president also travels on a helicopter. It is called Marine One. It may also be taken along when the president visits other countries.

★ Sometimes the president needs to get away with family and friends. Camp David is the official presidential retreat. It is located in Maryland. The US Navy maintains the retreat. The US Marine Corps keeps it secure. The camp offers swimming, tennis, golf, and hiking.

★ When the president leaves office, he or she receives lifetime Secret Service protection. He or she also receives a yearly pension of $203,700. The former president also receives money for office space, supplies, and staff.

33

PRESIDENTS AND THEIR TERMS

PRESIDENT	PARTY	TOOK OFFICE	LEFT OFFICE	TERMS SERVED	VICE PRESIDENT
George Washington	None	April 30, 1789	March 4, 1797	Two	John Adams
John Adams	Federalist	March 4, 1797	March 4, 1801	One	Thomas Jefferson
Thomas Jefferson	Democratic-Republican	March 4, 1801	March 4, 1809	Two	Aaron Burr, George Clinton
James Madison	Democratic-Republican	March 4, 1809	March 4, 1817	Two	George Clinton, Elbridge Gerry
James Monroe	Democratic-Republican	March 4, 1817	March 4, 1825	Two	Daniel D. Tompkins
John Quincy Adams	Democratic-Republican	March 4, 1825	March 4, 1829	One	John C. Calhoun
Andrew Jackson	Democrat	March 4, 1829	March 4, 1837	Two	John C. Calhoun, Martin Van Buren
Martin Van Buren	Democrat	March 4, 1837	March 4, 1841	One	Richard M. Johnson
William H. Harrison	Whig	March 4, 1841	April 4, 1841	Died During First Term	John Tyler
John Tyler	Whig	April 6, 1841	March 4, 1845	Completed Harrison's Term	Office Vacant
James K. Polk	Democrat	March 4, 1845	March 4, 1849	One	George M. Dallas
Zachary Taylor	Whig	March 5, 1849	July 9, 1850	Died During First Term	Millard Fillmore

PRESIDENT	PARTY	TOOK OFFICE	LEFT OFFICE	TERMS SERVED	VICE PRESIDENT
Millard Fillmore	Whig	July 10, 1850	March 4, 1853	Completed Taylor's Term	Office Vacant
Franklin Pierce	Democrat	March 4, 1853	March 4, 1857	One	William R.D. King
James Buchanan	Democrat	March 4, 1857	March 4, 1861	One	John C. Breckinridge
Abraham Lincoln	Republican	March 4, 1861	April 15, 1865	Served One Term, Died During Second Term	Hannibal Hamlin, Andrew Johnson
Andrew Johnson	Democrat	April 15, 1865	March 4, 1869	Completed Lincoln's Second Term	Office Vacant
Ulysses S. Grant	Republican	March 4, 1869	March 4, 1877	Two	Schuyler Colfax, Henry Wilson
Rutherford B. Hayes	Republican	March 3, 1877	March 4, 1881	One	William A. Wheeler
James A. Garfield	Republican	March 4, 1881	September 19, 1881	Died During First Term	Chester Arthur
Chester Arthur	Republican	September 20, 1881	March 4, 1885	Completed Garfield's Term	Office Vacant
Grover Cleveland	Democrat	March 4, 1885	March 4, 1889	One	Thomas A. Hendricks
Benjamin Harrison	Republican	March 4, 1889	March 4, 1893	One	Levi P. Morton
Grover Cleveland	Democrat	March 4, 1893	March 4, 1897	One	Adlai E. Stevenson
William McKinley	Republican	March 4, 1897	September 14, 1901	Served One Term, Died During Second Term	Garret A. Hobart, Theodore Roosevelt

PRESIDENT	PARTY	TOOK OFFICE	LEFT OFFICE	TERMS SERVED	VICE PRESIDENT
Theodore Roosevelt	Republican	September 14, 1901	March 4, 1909	Completed McKinley's Second Term, Served One Term	Office Vacant, Charles Fairbanks
William Taft	Republican	March 4, 1909	March 4, 1913	One	James S. Sherman
Woodrow Wilson	Democrat	March 4, 1913	March 4, 1921	Two	Thomas R. Marshall
Warren G. Harding	Republican	March 4, 1921	August 2, 1923	Died During First Term	Calvin Coolidge
Calvin Coolidge	Republican	August 3, 1923	March 4, 1929	Completed Harding's Term, Served One Term	Office Vacant, Charles Dawes
Herbert Hoover	Republican	March 4, 1929	March 4, 1933	One	Charles Curtis
Franklin D. Roosevelt	Democrat	March 4, 1933	April 12, 1945	Served Three Terms, Died During Fourth Term	John Nance Garner, Henry A. Wallace, Harry S. Truman
Harry S. Truman	Democrat	April 12, 1945	January 20, 1953	Completed Roosevelt's Fourth Term, Served One Term	Office Vacant, Alben Barkley
Dwight D. Eisenhower	Republican	January 20, 1953	January 20, 1961	Two	Richard Nixon
John F. Kennedy	Democrat	January 20, 1961	November 22, 1963	Died During First Term	Lyndon B. Johnson
Lyndon B. Johnson	Democrat	November 22, 1963	January 20, 1969	Completed Kennedy's Term, Served One Term	Office Vacant, Hubert H. Humphrey
Richard Nixon	Republican	January 20, 1969	August 9, 1974	Completed First Term, Resigned During Second Term	Spiro T. Agnew, Gerald Ford

PRESIDENT	PARTY	TOOK OFFICE	LEFT OFFICE	TERMS SERVED	VICE PRESIDENT
Gerald Ford	Republican	August 9, 1974	January 20, 1977	Completed Nixon's Second Term	Nelson A. Rockefeller
Jimmy Carter	Democrat	January 20, 1977	January 20, 1981	One	Walter Mondale
Ronald Reagan	Republican	January 20, 1981	January 20, 1989	Two	George H.W. Bush
George H.W. Bush	Republican	January 20, 1989	January 20, 1993	One	Dan Quayle
Bill Clinton	Democrat	January 20, 1993	January 20, 2001	Two	Al Gore
George W. Bush	Republican	January 20, 2001	January 20, 2009	Two	Dick Cheney
Barack Obama	Democrat	January 20, 2009	January 20, 2017	Two	Joe Biden

"In the councils of government, we must guard against the acquisition of unwarranted influence, whether sought or unsought, by the military-industrial complex." Dwight D. Eisenhower

★ WRITE TO THE PRESIDENT ★

You may write to the president at:
The White House
1600 Pennsylvania Avenue NW
Washington, DC 20500

You may e-mail the president at:
comments@whitehouse.gov

37

Glossary

academy—a private school that trains students in a certain field.

allies—people, groups, or nations working together. During World War II, Great Britain, France, the United States, and the Soviet Union were called the Allies.

civil rights—the rights of a citizen, such as the right to vote or freedom of speech.

Communism (KAHM-yuh-nih-zuhm)—a form of government in which all or most land and goods are owned by the state. They are then divided among the people based on need.

cure—a drug or some other treatment that ends an illness in a sick person.

Korean War—a war fought in North and South Korea from 1950 to 1953.

lieutenant—an officer of low rank in the armed forces.

NASA—National Aeronautics and Space Administration. NASA is run by the US government to study Earth, our solar system, and outer space.

NATO—North Atlantic Treaty Organization. A group formed by the United States, Canada, and some European countries that have agreed to give each other military help.

polio—the common name for poliomyelitis, a disease that sometimes leaves people paralyzed.

remedy—something that relieves pain, cures a disease, or corrects a disorder.

Republican—a member of the Republican political party.

satellite—a spacecraft sent into orbit around a heavenly body.

secretary of health and human services—a member of the president's cabinet who handles national health matters.

segregate—to separate a person or a group from a larger group.

spy—someone who secretly collects information about an enemy or competitor.

surrender—to give up.

World War II—a war fought in Europe, Asia, and Africa from 1939 to 1945.

WEBSITES ★ ★

To learn more about the US Presidents, visit **booklinks.abdopublishing.com**. These links are routinely monitored and updated to provide the most current information available.

Index